The Church Within the Church

McDougal & Associates
*Servants of Christ and Stewards of
the Mysteries of God*

The Church Within the Church

by

Phyllis Harper Isenhart

The Church Within the Church
Copyright © 2025—Phyllis Harper Isenhart
ALL RIGHTS RESERVED

Bible references marked "KJV" are from the *Holy Bible, King James Version*. References marked "NIV" are from the *Holy Bible, New International Version,* copyright © 1973, 1978, 1984, 2011 by Biblica, Colorado Springs, Colorado. References marked "NKJV" are from *The Holy Bible, New King James Version*, copyright © 1979, 1980, 1982, 1990 by Thomas Nelson, Inc., Nashville, Tennessee. References marked "NASB" are from the *New American Standard Bible*, copyright © 1960, 1962, 1963, 1968, 1971, 1972, 1973, 1975, 1977 by the Lockman Foundation, La Habra, California. References marked NABRE are from the *New American Bible,* revised edition copyright © 2010, 1991, 1986, 1970 Confraternity of Christian Doctrine, Inc., Washington, DC. All rights reserved. Used by Permission.

McDougal & Associates is dedicated to spreading the Gospel of the Lord Jesus Christ to as many people as possible in the shortest time possible.

Published by:

McDougal & Associates
www.ThePublishedWord.com

ISBN: 978-1-964665-40-5

Printed on demand in the U.S., the U.K., Australia
For Worldwide Distribution

Dedication

I dedicate this work, first and foremost, to Jesus Christ, the One who left the ninety-nine to go find me. He is the One who picked me up out of a mirey pit and set my feet upon a firm foundation. He is the One who walks with me and talks with me and loves me in spite of all my failings. Without Him, I would not be the person I am today.

Father God, I thank You for Your Son and Your precious Holy Spirit. You are my life!

To the many who have gone before me, who plowed the ground for me to walk on, grow in, and learn from, whose shoulders I stand on, thank you for your labor. It was not in vain.

Acknowledgments

There have been many down through the years who have had a profound impact on my life—my parents, my children, pastors, teachers, and close friends. There are several I want to acknowledge with special recognition in reference to this work.

To **Betsy Roy** for planting the seed for this message in my spirit. A simple phrase you posted one morning in a prayer group dropped into my spirit and took root. Thank you, Betsy, for the title of this work, and thank you for your devotion to the Kingdom of God.

To my Pastor, **Timothy Cavenaugh**, for your obedience in allowing the Spirit to use you to get my butt busy doing what I knew I was to do but was dragging my feet. Your words were taken to heart and are bearing fruit. Thank you for your words of encouragement.

To my editor, **Prophetess and Teacher Nkenge Tuck**, you are the best. Your wisdom and knowledge of the Word inspire me to be a better person and to go deeper in Christ. When you find someone you can spend six hours at a whack talking and laughing with and not even realize that amount of time has flown by, you have found a family member. Thank you for being, not only a friend, but also a sister. Love you!

For my cover design, **Danielle Cox**, graphic designer and media artist, thank you for a beautiful cover photo. I love the way it pops. You are the best. May God richly bless you in all your endeavors.

I am jealous for you with a godly jealousy. I promised you to one husband, to Christ, so that I might present you as a pure virgin to him. But I am afraid that just as Eve was deceived by the serpent's cunning, your minds may somehow be led astray from your sincere and pure devotion to Christ.
— 2 Corinthians 11:2-3, NIV

Contents

1. The Church Within a Church 11

2. The Growth of the Church 15

3. The Early Church 17

4. Abraham, the Father of Faith 31

5. God's Purpose 35

6. The Decline of the Church 46

7. The True Church 50

8. Fruit Versus Gifts of the Spirit 61

9. The Final Church 71

About the Author 81

Other Books by Phyllis Isenhart 85

**Let us rejoice and be glad
 and give him glory!
For the wedding of
 the Lamb has come,
 and his bride has
made herself ready.
Fine linen, bright and
clean,
 was given her to
wear."**

**(Fine linen stands for the righteous acts of God's holy people.)
—Revelation 19:7-8, NIV**

1

The Church Within a Church

The Church within a church ... say what? What are you talking about? A Church within a church? How can that be? I've never heard of such a thing. In this book, I hope to be able to shed some light on this subject in a way you can understand, using the Word of God.

Let's begin with what exactly the church is. The church, contrary to the thinking of many, is not the building we go to every week, and it is not the services or meetings we attend in that building. The building is simply that, a building or a place to gather. Basket-

The Church Within the Church

ball fans gather in a gym to watch their team play. Believers in Jesus gather in a building we call a church building, but it is just a building.

Matthew 16 is the first place in the New Testament that references the church. In this passage, Jesus asked His disciples:

> *"Who do you say I am?"*
> *Simon Peter answered, "You are the Messiah, the Son of the living God."*
> *[Jesus replied to Simon], "And I tell you that you are Peter [petros in Greek], and on this rock I will build my church [ekklesia in Greek], and the gates of Hades [Hell] will not overcome it."*
> Matthew 16:15-16 and 18, NIV

Petros in Greek means "rock," and a rock is hard. It was Simon Peter's faith in the revelation of who Jesus is that was rock solid. Jesus was saying it was that type of faith that His Church would be built on. The Greek word for

The Church Within a Church

church is *ekklesia*, and is a combination of *"ek"* (Strongs #1537) meaning "origin (the point where motion begins)" and *kaleo* (Strongs #2564) akin to *keleuo* #2753, meaning "a cry or an incitement." Another variant is *ekklektos*, meaning "called-out one," hence we get the term *Church* as the called-out ones for Christ.

"And I tell you that you are Peter [petros in Greek], and on this rock I will build my church [ekklesia in Greek], and the gates of Hades [Hell] will not overcome it!"

2

The Growth of the Church

In the first century, as the Good News, the Gospel, began to spread and grow, Gentiles from outside Jerusalem were being saved and filled with the Holy Ghost. As this news reached the Church in Jerusalem, the elders sent Barnabas to Antioch to see if what they were hearing was true. Barnabas discovered that it was true and went to find Paul. Once he found Paul, he took him back to Antioch, and Paul and Barnabas stayed at Antioch for a year teaching the people. Acts 11:26 says these new disciples were called *Christians* first at Antioch.

These new disciples were called **Christians** first at Antioch!

3

The Early Church

The Church has evolved dramatically over the last two thousand years, but unfortunately, interpretations have been skewed and man's view and beliefs have made their way in, thus dividing the Church, with whole denominations built as beliefs became rules and regulations. In the process, the Scriptures were taken out of context and taught as gospel truth. In many groups, the Scriptures have been watered down in order to appease the common culture. These changes didn't all happen at once, but over the years, a little at a time, one thought, one idea, one belief, one rule or

The Church Within the Church

regulation at a time. Little by little, people began to accept these ideas because they trusted their leadership. The same thing goes for today. So, you might ask, "Where does this lead and how do we know?" Better yet, "How do we fix it?"

First, I would like to take you on a journey or history lesson beginning at the *"ek"* beginning. The Israelites were God's chosen people. He chose them, they didn't choose Him. As a matter of fact, when they were slaves in Egypt, God chose Moses, a stutterer, to lead His people out.

At first, things seemed to be going well. However, it was not long before the people grew restless waiting for Moses who had gone up on a mountain to pray, and they decided to go back to their old ways and habits. They got Aaron, Moses' brother, to make a golden calf for them to worship. This type of idolatry had been going on as long as mankind had been on the earth.

The Scriptures were taken out of context and taught as gospel truth, and, in many groups, the Scriptures have been watered down in order to appease the common culture!

The Church Within the Church

Genesis 6:5-7 states:

Then the LORD saw that the wickedness of mankind was great in the earth, and that every intent of the thoughts of their heart was only evil continually. So the LORD was sorry that He had made mankind on the earth, and He was grieved in His heart. Then the LORD said, "I will wipe out mankind whom I have created from the face of the land; mankind, and animals as well, and crawling things, and the birds of the sky. For I am sorry that I have made them." (NASB)

So, God found Moses, a murderer, who had run from his crime and was hiding on the backside of the desert, to go lead the people out of captivity in Egypt. However, because of their rebellion, they spent the next forty years travelling what should have been approximately 250 miles to get to the Promised Land.

The Early Church

Once they finally made it there, instead of following God's laws, they began to accept the culture of those around them, accepting their evil practices and even started worshipping their pagan gods instead of Yahweh. Jeremiah 17:9 states:

The heart is deceitful above all things, and desperately wicked. (KJV)

It has always been this way, and that is why we need a Savior. Mankind is incapable of saving himself. Father God knew this from the beginning, so He decided to take a part of Himself and go down and save man. God's purpose for mankind was to have a family that loved Him from their heart, not for what He could do for them, but for who He was and is.

God tried to get His people to turn back to Him. He sent messengers and prophets to warn them, but would they listen? No, they hardened their hearts even more. So, finally Father God decided that the time was right and sent His only Son into the

Father God knew this from the beginning, so He decided to take a part of Himself and go down and save man. His purpose for mankind was to have a family that loved Him from their heart, not for what He could do for them, but for who He was and is!

The Early Church

world. And so, enters Jesus, the Anointed One, on the scene.

Jesus walked among His people doing what His Father asked Him to do. He taught, performed miracles, and healed many. Many of those He encountered followed Him, but the religious leaders of the day refused Him. However, God had a plan, and that plan was that every person would be saved. His heart was not only for a family that loved Him, but also loved each other. So, Jesus called together a group of twelve men to teach and instill in the hearts of the people the love and plan of Abba Father.

Jesus mentored these disciples for three years, preparing them to carry His love and message to the whole world. Then Jesus, knowing that His time on earth was about to end, called His twelve disciples together and point blank asked them, *"Who do you say that I am?"* Simon very boldly declared, *"You are the Messiah, the Son of the living God."* Jesus then told His disciples that upon that

The Church Within the Church

revelation He would build His Church (*ekklesia*).

Not long after this, Jesus was crucified and buried, and three days later He rose to life again, but He soon ascended back to Heaven. This left the responsibility of carrying the Good News to others squarely on the shoulders of the disciples.

Before Jesus left, He appeared to His disciples and instructed them to not leave Jerusalem, but to wait for the gift His Father had promised, which He had already told them about. As they were questioning Jesus about when, where, and how this would all happen, Jesus replied:

> *It is not for you to know the times or dates the Father has set by his own authority. But you will receive power when the Holy Spirit comes on you; and you will be my witnesses in Jerusalem, and in all Judea and Samaria and to the ends of the earth.*
> Acts 1:7-8 (NIV)

God had a plan, and that plan was that every person would be saved!

The Church Within the Church

After He had said this, He was taken up before their very eyes, and a cloud hid him from their sight.
Verse 9 (NIV)

The disciples, now apostles or sent ones, returned from the Mount of Olives, where they had just witnessed Jesus taken up in a cloud, to Jerusalem to the room where they were staying. They agreed to choose someone to fill the vacancy created by Judas' betrayal, so they chose Matthias.

On the Day of Pentecost, there were about one hundred and twenty people gathered in that upper room. As they were praising and worshipping God, suddenly a sound like a violent wind blew in and filled the room. As they looked around to see what was happening, they saw what looked like tongues of fire that separated and rested on each person. They were all filled with the Holy Spirit and began speaking in other languages as they were enabled by the Holy Spirit.

They were all filled with the Holy Spirit and began speaking in other languages as they were enabled by the Holy Spirit!

The Church Within the Church

Because this happened during the Jewish feast of Pentecost, there were people from many different nations in Jerusalem. Hearing this noise from that upper room, people gathered outside and were amazed that they were hearing in their own language. They questioned how these men, who were Galileans, were able to speak in their native language and declare the wonders of God so that each could understand it.

As some were claiming that the disciples were drunk, Simon, who was now called Peter, stood up and addressed the crowd, telling them about Jesus. Because of that message, approximately three thousand believed and were baptized. Thus, the Church was born.

With so many being added daily, the apostles decided they needed some help to meet all the needs of the people, so that the apostles could concentrate on prayer and fasting. They chose a man named Stephen. At this time, there was much opposition to those followers of

The Early Church

Jesus, now known as *The Way*. Stephen was accused of blasphemy and called to appear before the Sanhedrin Court, he was convicted and sentenced to be stoned to death.

As Stephen was being stoned, there was a young man named Saul standing nearby watching. After that, Saul, who was adamantly against those of The Way, went around threatening and arresting many. But as he was on his way to Damascus to hunt down believers, he had a personal encounter with the risen Jesus and was himself converted. At this time, God changed Saul's name to Paul. Through Paul the Church began to grow even more and spread throughout the region and, through the centuries, it has covered the entire world.

They questioned how these men, who were Galileans, were able to speak in their native language and declare the wonders of God so that each could understand it!

4

Abraham, the Father of Faith

As noted, from the very beginning, God's desire was to have a family that would love Him for who He was and is, not for what He would do for them or what they could get from Him. God searched until He found the man He wanted. That man's name was Abraham. He chose Abraham and made a covenant with him. This covenant, now widely known as the Abrahamic Covenant, was an unconditional covenant or agreement between God and Abraham and consisted of four parts or elements: land, descendants, blessing, and a sign. God promised Abraham and his descendants the land of Canaan, later to become Israel. God promised Abraham countless descendants, as countless as the stars in the sky or the sand on the seashore. God promised to bless Abraham and, through him, all the families of the earth would be blessed. Lastly, as a sign of this covenant, God commanded Abraham and his male descendants to be circumcised.

It was Abraham's descendants, Isaac and Jacob, that this covenant was passed down through. As Jacob was on his way back to Canaan from Panddan Aram, he stopped at the ford of the Jabbok River. While there, Jacob wrestled with a man till daybreak. When the man asked Jacob to let him go, Jacob replied, *"Not unless you bless me."* The man asked what his name was, and Jacob told him. The man then said:

> *Your name will no longer be Jacob, but Israel, because you have struggled with God and with humans and have overcome.* Genesis 32:28 (NIV)

Your name will no longer be Jacob, but Israel, because you have struggled with God and with humans and have overcome!

The Church Within the Church

Thus, the nation of Israel was born, the covenant being passed down from Jacob/Israel though his twelve sons.

Fast forward a few thousand years, and we find a man named Joseph, a descendant of Judah, son of Jacob. Joseph was engaged to Mary when she miraculously became pregnant by the Holy Spirit. She gave birth to a Baby Boy, and they named Him Jesus. It was this same Jesus who was crucified. and the disciples watched as He went back to His Father in the clouds.

5

God's Purpose

Again, from the beginning, God's desire was for a family that loved Him. That purpose came from God's love. God loved His creation, but His prized creation was man. He created Adam and Eve with a will or choice. God did not want a puppet family but a people that willingly chose to serve Him. That purpose has not changed, and neither has mankind.

Under the Abrahamic Covenant, God laid out to the children of Israel laws and regulations which they were to live by. However, they, in their selfish nature, chose to do what they wanted instead. Their desire was to be like the nations

God loved His creation, but His prized creation was man. He created Adam and Eve with a will or choice. God did not want a puppet family but a people that willingly chose to serve Him!

God's Purpose

living around them. They wanted to be accepted and to blend in. We, today, are no different. We do the same thing. We want to be accepted; no one likes rejection. That is our human nature. And we have difficulty believing in anything we can't see. Therefore, believing in an invisible God is unnatural to man. We forget to recognize that, as well as being human, we are also spiritual beings. It is that spiritual part that God is concerned about. When we die, our bodies will decay and go back to the dust from which they are made. The spirit and soul, on the other hand, will never die, but will live forever.

Jesus came to redeem (buy back or save) the soul and spirit of fallen men. Human flesh has its own desires, and those desires are at enmity with God. Jesus' life as fully man is our example of how to live. That was another of His purposes for leaving His Father and coming to earth, to be the example, to show mankind how to live.

The Church Within the Church

Man's inherent nature is to be in control. We were created that way by God, our Creator. God gave us a will, and He won't override that will. You might ask, "Why?" And that's a good question. God does not want a puppet family, but one that chooses to be part of His family, one that will choose to follow the family rules that the Father has set down. Father always knows best.

Down through the years, man, by his inherent nature, has tried and, in many cases, succeeded in manipulating and dictating *his* will and *his* interpretation of what the church should be. It was this type of manipulation that ushered in the divisions into different man-made denominations.

One example is the relevance of the Holy Spirit. Some say what happened in Acts chapter 2 is no longer relevant, that it stopped when the last disciple of Jesus died. Some believe that Mary, the mother of Jesus, and some of the apostles have divine powers. Others

Down through the years, man, by his inherent nature, has tried and, in many cases, succeeded in manipulating and dictating his will and his interpretation of what the church should be!

The Church Within the Church

want to put dress restrictions on who can become a member of the church. These man-made rules and regulations are no different from what the religious leaders did in Jesus' day. Some say that if you are of a different race or skin color, you are better or worse than others.

Isaiah 1:11-20 gives us God's feelings and thoughts about man's ways of worship. "But didn't God ordain the sacrifices and feast?" you might ask. Yes, He did, but it was to remind the Israelites of their need for a Savior. Instead, the people began to look on these rituals as their Savior, thinking it was the bull or the goat that forgave their sins and iniquities.

> *To what purpose is the multitude of*
> *your sacrifices to Me?"*
> *Says the* L<small>ORD</small>.
> *I have had enough of burnt offerings*
> *of rams*
> *And the fat of fed cattle.*

God's Purpose

I do not delight in the blood of bulls,
Or of lambs or goats.
When you come to appear before Me,
Who has required this from your hand,
To trample My courts?
Bring no more futile sacrifices;
Incense is an abomination to Me.
The New Moons, the Sabbaths and the calling of assemblies —
I cannot endure iniquity and the sacred meeting.
Your New Moons and your appointed feast
My soul hates;
They are a trouble to Me.
I am weary of hearing them.
When you spread out your hands,
I will hide my eyes from you;
Even though you make many prayers,
I will not hear.
Your hands are full of blood.

Wash yourselves, make yourselves clean;

The Church Within the Church

Put away the evil of your doing from before My eyes.
Cease to do evil,
Learn to do good;
Seek justice,
Rebuke the oppressor,
Defend the fatherless,
Plead for the widow.

"Come now and let us reason together," says the LORD.
"Though your sins are like scarlet,
They shall be as white as snow;
Though they are red like crimson,
They shall be as wool.
If you are willing and obedient,
You will eat the good of the land;
But if you refuse and rebel, you shall be devoured by the sword";
For the mouth of the LORD has spoken. Isaiah 1:11-20 (NKJV)

God is not impressed with our heartless or halfhearted worship.

Wash yourselves, make yourselves clean;
Put away the evil of your doing from before My eyes.
Cease to do evil,
Learn to do good;
Seek justice,
Rebuke the oppressor,
Defend the fatherless,
Plead for the widow!

The Church Within the Church

What He wants is a heart of worship. He said:

> *My son give attention to My words;*
> *Incline your ear to My sayings.*
> *Do not let them depart from your eyes;*
> *Keep them in the midst of your heart;*
> *For they are life to those who find them,*
> *And health to all their flesh.*
> *Keep your heart with all diligence,*
> *For out of it spring the issues of life.*
> *Put away from you a deceitful mouth,*
> *And put perverse lips far from you.*
> *Let your eyes look straight ahead,*
> *And your eyelids look right before you.*
> *Ponder the path of your feet,*
> *And let all your ways be established.*
> Proverbs 4:20-26 (NKJV)

"Come now and let us reason together," says the Lord. "Though your sins are like scarlet, They shall be as white as snow; Though they are red like crimson, They shall be as wool. If you are willing and obedient, You will eat the good of the land; But if you refuse and rebel, you shall be devoured by the sword!"

6

The Decline of the Church

Many ask, "What happened to bring about the slow decline the church has experienced?" I would say that one of the major factors began taking hold in the 1940s and early 1950s when the push for the separation of Church and State began to surface. Certain nonbelievers decided that God should have no place in our government, and they began to push that agenda. That same group then pushed to have prayer removed from public schools and demanded that anything having to do with religion be disallowed. Once this was accomplished, they now had control over the next generation.

The Decline of the Church

The next step was the family unit. If the family unit could be broken up, then so goes the Church. We must understand that the author of all this is Satan. Satan is the one behind this decline. He couldn't win over Jesus, so he wants to destroy the Church. There are three things that the Bible warns us of: the lust of the flesh, the lust of the eye, and the pride of life. All these three are rooted in human nature.

The lust of the flesh has to do with our physical desires and encompasses a wide range of desires such as sexual desires, sexual immorality, sensual desires that if given into will lead to sin such as anger and jealousy. The lust of the eye is the desire for material possessions or seeking external appearances or fixating on things we see with our eyes or on our wants, that which is visibly appealing. The pride of life is the desire or inclination for self-exaltation. It can manifest itself in several ways, such as a desire for personal glory, a desire for power or

If the family unit could be broken up, then so goes the Church!

The Decline of the Church

for material possessions. All of these are diametrically opposed to God's way of life by denying God's role in our lives.

If any one of these are allowed to become rooted in our lives, we shut the door for God to bless us and draw us closer to Him, thus depending on ourselves. When we bring this attitude into the church, it causes rifts and divisions in the Body of Christ. Our desire must submit to and come into alignment with God's desires. The apostle Paul, in his letters to the different churches in the region, addressed many of these same issues and instructed the leaders in how to deal with these issues. The nature of man has not changed and will not until it submits to God. Until we acknowledge out sinful nature, we will fight against the ways of God, even in the church.

The True Church

The Bible lays out for us the hierarchy or foundational structure of God's Church through Paul's epistles:

And he gave some, apostles; and some, prophets; and some, evangelists; and some, pastors and teachers; for the perfecting of the saints, for the work of the ministry, for the edifying of the body of Christ: till we all come in the unity of the faith, and of the knowledge of the Son of God, unto a perfect man, unto the measure of the stature of the fulness of Christ: that we henceforth be no more children, tossed to and fro, and

The True Church

carried about with every wind of doctrine, by the sleight of men, and cunning craftiness, whereby they lie in wait to deceive; but speaking the truth in love, may grow up into him in all things, which is the head, even Christ: from whom the whole body fitly joined together and compacted by that which every joint supplieth, according to the effectual working in the measure of every part, maketh increase of the body unto the edifying of itself in love.
     Ephesians 4:11-16 (KJV)

Apostles – The word *apostle* means "one who is sent out" to be a messenger or ambassador of Jesus Christ, to spread the Gospel. There is much debate about whether or not apostles are still relevant today. Matthew 28:18, known as the Great Commission, commands us to go and make disciples of all nations. Today some would call them missionaries, but they are sent ones.

For the perfecting of the saints,
For the work of the ministry,
For the edifying of the body of Christ:
Til we all come in the unity of the faith, and of the knowledge of the Son of God,
Unto a perfect man,
Unto the measure of the stature of the fulness of Christ!

The True Church

We are therefore Christ's ambassadors, as though God were making his appeal through us. We implore you on Christ's behalf: Be reconciled to God. 2 Corinthians 5:20 (NIV)

Prophets – The word *prophet* means "a person who speaks for God or a deity, or by divine inspiration." According to *Merrian-Webster*, the definition is:

- One who utters divinely inspired revelations
- One gifted with more than ordinary spiritual and moral insight
- One who foretells future events
- An effective or leading spokesman for a cause, doctrine, or group

We know that the Bible is the complete and authoritative Word of God. Some would argue that because the Bible is the final Word, there is no need today for prophets. If that were true, why would they be given as a gift to

The Church Within the Church

the Church? Let's explore that question.

We know and understand that the Bible can be hard to understand. That's why we have so many different versions. Even with new versions, it can be difficult to understand what is really being said. We also understand that the same language differs in different areas of the world. Also, our lifestyles have changed over the centuries, and cultures have changed. But God's Word never changes. It is, like Jesus, the same yesterday, today, and forever.

Prophets can speak to us or to our situation with clarity from God in a way that we can understand and comprehend. They help equip believers to discern God's voice and live according to biblical truth rather than worldly or false advice. However, any word spoken over an individual claiming to be a prophet must align with the Bible, God's Word.

God's Word never changes. It is, like Jesus, the same yesterday, today, and forever!

The Church Within the Church

Evangelists – The word *evangelist* refers to "a person who speaks to convert others to Christ or the Christian faith, especially by public preaching or speaking." We get this word *evangelist* from the Greek word *euggelistes*, meaning "a bringing of good tidings." All of us, as believers, can and should be moving in this gift, for the world is looking and hoping for good news.

There is a saying: We are the only Bible some people will ever read. This means that our lives and speech should reflect the Gospel and the goodness of God. We are to share with others what God has done for us.

Pastors – A pastor is "a spiritual leader within a Christian congregation." A pastor's primary duties include preaching, teaching, counseling, and offering spiritual guidance. The term comes from the Hebrew word *mirah*, which means "pasture" and refers to a place for grazing or feeding animals. The pastor is the shep-

A pastor's primary duties include preaching, teaching, counseling, and offering spiritual guidance!

herd of the flock. Pastors are responsible for delivering sermons and teaching biblical doctrine to their congregations. They are also to provide pastoral care to individuals in their congregation, addressing their spiritual and, sometimes, even their physical needs. The pastor is also to oversee the direction of the local congregation, insuring that it aligns with the vision God has given for that congregation. Therefore, prayer is also a major aspect of their duties.

Teachers – A teacher is a person who imparts or helps others to acquire knowledge, competence, and values. Teacher is a designation for the office, position, or profession of a person who devotes him- or herself to education through interaction, formal or casual and systematic. A teacher can also be a mentor who facilitates learning, inspires others, and shapes their knowledge, skills, and values for success in life.

The True Church

In Ephesians 4:16, Paul groups pastors and teachers together as a combined office. However, there are distinct differences. While all pastors are teachers of God's Word, all teachers are not pastors. One of the major differences is in the focus. The main focus of the pastor is to nurture, guide, and care for the spiritual well-being of the flock. The main focus of the teacher is to explain and illuminate the truth of God's Word in a clear and understandable way.

The goal of each is also different. The goal of the pastor is to bring people into spiritual maturity and faithful living, while that of a teacher is to impart knowledge and equip people with a deeper understand of biblical truth. All of these five offices are essential for growth and maturity in the Body of believers.

The main focus of the pastor is to nurture, guide, and care for the spiritual well-being of the flock. The main focus of the teacher is to explain and illuminate the truth of God's Word in a clear and understandable way!

Fruit Versus Gifts of the Holy Spirit

Another area where there are major differences within the church is concerning the gifts of the Spirit and fruits of the Spirit. I would like to dive into the fruits of Spirit first. Paul wrote:

> *Now the Lord is the Spirit, and where the Spirit of the Lord is, there is freedom: and we all, who with unveiled faces contemplate [or reflect] the Lord's glory, are being transformed into his image with ever-increasing glory, which comes from the Lord, who is the Spirit.*
> 2 Corinthians 3:17-18 (NIV)

Now the Lord is the Spirit, and where the Spirit of the Lord is, there is freedom!

Fruit Versus Gifts of the Holy Spirit

Before we accepted Christ, we had a veil, so to speak, over our eyes and our hearts, preventing us from seeing and understanding the Gospel, the love and goodness of God. When we accepted Christ and were born again, that veil was lifted from us and we became a new creation. Now the Spirit can work in us. This work can sometimes be a slow process, depending on how willing we are to be pruned of our old ways and habits. It is during this process that the Holy Spirit begins to develop His fruit in us.

Galatians 5:13-22 talks about living life in the Spirit:

> *You, my brothers and sisters, were called to be free, but do not use your freedom to indulge in the flesh, rather serve one another humbly in love. For the entire law is fulfilled in keeping this one command: Love you neighbor as yourself.*
> *"*   Verses 13-14 (NIV)

The Church Within the Church

Verses 22 and 23 list the fruits of the Spirit as *"love, joy, peace, forbearance, kindness, goodness, faithfulness, gentleness and self-control."* Jesus said:

> *By their fruit you will know them.*
> Matthew 7:16 (NABRE)

Here He was talking about false prophets, but this truth can also apply to people in general. Out of the heart the mouth speaks, actions are made, and deeds are done.

The fruits of the Spirit are cultivated in us as we grow and mature in our walk with Christ. The gifts, however, are different. They are given by God through the Holy Spirit. Since they are gifts, they are given as He chooses.

The gifts of the Spirit are supernatural abilities given to edify or minister to the Church and/or the individual. Paul speaks of these in 1 Corinthians 12. Here he lists the nine gifts, which are classified into three categories: the power to

Do not use your freedom to indulge in the flesh, rather serve one another humbly in love!

know supernaturally, the power to act supernaturally, and the power to speak supernaturally.

The first set, the power to know supernaturally, would be (a) the word of wisdom, (b) the word of knowledge, and (c) discernment. The word of wisdom seems to signify the supernatural ability to utter wisdom concerning certain situations or problems. The word of knowledge is the ability to supernaturally utter facts that the person uttering it would not normally have knowledge of. So, what is the difference between a word of wisdom and a word of knowledge? Myer Pearlman wrote, "Knowledge is insight to divine things, and wisdom is the skill which regulates the Christian life according to its foundational principles."[1]

Discerning of Spirits is the ability to supernaturally know if a person or prophet is speaking by the Spirit of God or out of his or her own spirit. This gift <u>enables the</u> possessor to see through all

---

1. *Knowing the Doctrines of the Bible* by Myer Pearlman, Gospel Publishing House, Springfield, Missouri: 1981

Discerning of Spirits is the ability to supernaturally know if a person or prophet is speaking by the Spirit of God or out of his or her own spirit!

outward appearances and know the true nature of inspiration.

The second set of gifts, the power to act supernaturally, are (a) gift of faith, (b) gifts of healing, and (c) the working of miracles. The gift of faith is different from saving faith. It is a special, supernatural ability to trust God completely and totally for a specific task or in a difficult situation or circumstance. The gifts of healing is a supernatural ability to minister health to the sick through prayer. The working of miracles is the supernatural power to perform miracles.

The third set of gifts, the power to speak, are (a) prophecy, (b) speaking in tongues, and (c) the interpretation of tongues. Prophecy is speaking forth God's oracles or message and is used to edify, build up, and encourage others and, sometimes, to reveal future events. Speaking in tongues is the supernatural ability to speak in a language unknown to the speaker. This can be used to get the attention of others or direct personal

Fruit Versus Gifts of the Holy Spirit

communication with God. The Interpretation of tongues is the supernatural ability to understand, interpret, and explain a message given in tongues, allowing that message to edify the Body of Christ.

There are many beliefs and opinions within the Church as to whether these nine gifts are still active and viable today. Many mainstream denominations believe these ceased with the first century church. However, the Bible tells us that God is the same yesterday, today, and forever. He does not change. So, we see that everyone should produce the fruits of the Spirit, but God, in His infinite wisdom, dispenses His gifts however and to whomever He sees fit and at His own discretion.

God, in His infinite wisdom, dispenses His gifts however and to whomever He sees fit and at His own discretion!

9

The Final Church

So, now the big question is: what does the Church look like and who will make up the church at the end of the age? Jesus, in Matthew 15:8-9, quotes a passage from Isaiah 29:13:

These people come near to me with their mouth
 and honor me with their lips,
 but their hearts are far from me.
Their worship of me
 is based on merely human rules
they have been taught. (NIV)

In John 4:23-24, Jesus gives us a glimpse of what He is looking for from us. He told the Samaritan woman at the well:

> *Yet a time is coming and has now come when the true worshipper will worship the Father in the Spirit and truth, for they are the kind of worshippers the Father seeks. God is spirit, and his worshippers must worship him in Spirit and truth.*
>
> (NIV)

Years ago I heard Evangelist David Alsobrook, when teaching on The Precious Blood, refer to worshipping in Spirit and truth as worshipping "in Spirit and reality." That phrase stuck with me, and I believe it needs to be applied in this day and time. We are living right now in a world where good is considered evil, and evil is considered good. That mindset seems to be portrayed as truth, but it is not that way. Let's look at those two terms.

Webster defines *truth* as "conformable to fact, in accordance with the actual state of things, correct, not false, erroneous, or inaccurate." So then, truth is "stating" what is true. *Webster* defines reality as "(1) the state or quality of being real, actual being or existence of anything, in distinction from mere appearance; fact (2) that which is real; and actual existence; that which is not imagined, fiction or pretense; that which has objective existence and is not merely an idea." We are living in a world where truth is being distorted, and that distortion is finding its way into the church and being accepted as truth. The truth is that sin is sin in the eyes of God, and Jesus came to take away the sin of the world (see John 1:29). Here and in other passages, sin is considered as missing the mark or as disobedience or deviating from obedience to God's character and will.

When people recognize what is not real as being true, they are believing a lie. The Bible is true, and the reality of that truth must be applied as such in

The Church Within the Church

life. It must become real in our hearts and our lives. The Church must stand on the truth of God's Word because that is what is real, the reality of life.

There are those who attend church every week but live and do as they please, with no regard to God's desire. They believe on and accept Christ, but they never grow and mature in their walk. God sees their heart, but He is searching for those who have accepted Christ, have had their hearts circumcised, and whose lives are aligned with His Holy Word. It is those, my beloved, who make up the Church within the church.

The Church is the Body of Christ. In the beginning, in the garden, when God first created man, He said it was not good that man should be alone, and He created a helpmeet for him, a woman taken from his side. He then presented her to Adam, and their's was the first marriage. In Ephesians 5:25-33, the Bible likens the earthly marriage of a man and woman to the union of Christ and His

There are those who attend church every week but live and do as they please, with no regard to God's desire. They believe on and accept Christ, but they never grow and mature in their walk!

The Church Within the Church

Church, His marriage to the Bride of Christ. Verse 27 states:

> *That He might present her [His Bride] to Himself a glorious church, not having spot or wrinkle or any such thing, but that she should be holy and without blemish. (NKJV).*

Having no stain is being free from any impurities or being immaculate. No wrinkles signifies no defects or flaws.

In the Parable of the Ten Virgins, we see another illustration. The ten virgins were all waiting for the bridegroom to come. They had all brought oil for their lamps. However, five had brought extra oil and five had not. We know that oil is symbolic of the Holy Spirit. When the bridegroom came, the five who had not brought extra oil ran out and had to leave to get more, and therefore, they were not present when the bridegroom came. They were not fully prepared. The Holy Spirit is the one who cleanses us

The Final Church

and purifies us and gets us ready for the Groom. Revelation 19:7 declares:

*Let us rejoice and be glad
  and give him glory!
For the wedding of the Lamb has come,
  and his bride has made herself ready.* (NIV)

Everyone who has accepted Christ will be at the wedding, but those in the Church who have their lamps (lives) filled with oil will become the Bride.

Matthew 22:1-14 gives us the Parable of the Wedding Banquet. The king sent out invitations for a wedding banquet for his son. Many who received an invitation made excuses as to why they could not attend and went off to do their own thing. He then sent out his servants to compel others to come in. When the king came in to greet the guests, there was a man there who was not wearing wedding garments (not dressed prop-

Everyone who has accepted Christ will be at the wedding, but those in the Church who have their lamps (lives) filled with oil will become the Bride!

The Final Church

erly). The king asked, "How did you get in here without the proper wedding garments?" The man could not answer, so the king told his servants to tie him hand and foot and throw him out into the darkness.

My question to you is this: Will you be part of the Bride who is dressed in fine linen, will you be merely a participant invited to the banquet dinner, or will you be one who gets thrown out because you refused the invitation or failed to dress yourself in the correct wedding apparel? My friend, I pray that you will make the right decision today.

Will you be part of the Bride who is dressed in fine linen, will you be merely a participant invited to the banquet dinner, or will you be one who gets thrown out because you refused the invitation or failed to dress yourself in the correct wedding apparel?

About the Author

Phyllis Harper Isenhart was born November 4, 1947 in eastern North Carolina, the third of four children born to Saint Elmo and Nancy Willis Harper. Yes, although he went by Elmo, Saint was her father's given first name at birth. He was a Free Will Baptist preacher and pastor, so from the time she was born, she was carried to church. In June of 1958, she accepted Christ as her personal Savior and was baptized in water.

Phyllis graduated high school and went on to college for a while. For the next ten years, however, she did her own thing. In 1970 she married a marine, and together they had four children. By 1984, she found herself in a legal separation, which finally ended in divorce in 1996.

The Church Within the Church

Phyllis went to church off and on but was never happy with the result. Then, in March of 1979, while the family was living in Beaufort, South Carolina, her two older children began urging her to go to church with them. They had been riding a church bus for about a year and one particular Sunday if they brought a visitor with them, they would get to fish a gift out of a pool. For several weeks, they begged her to go, until she finally relented and said okay.

Phyllis was not immediately aware of the fact that this was the very same church she had attended a couple of years before and had vowed never to go back. As it turned out, it was the same church building, but it was not the same church. They had changed pastors in the meantime. That Sunday became her new spiritual birthday. She surrendered her life to Christ and decided to follow Him all the days of her life.

Now Phyllis was like a sponge. She simply could not get enough of God. That May she was baptized in the Holy

About the Author

Ghost, and for the next three years, she sat under the teaching of Rev. Gaylon and Barbara Benton, who became her mentors and very dear friends.

In December of 1981, Phyllis' husband was transferred to Camp Lejeune, North Carolina, and there she was introduced to an Assembly of God church in Jacksonville, which she began to attend. It was during this time that her marriage began to fall apart, and her whole world seemed to fall apart with it. One day, while she was at her very lowest point, she was sitting on her couch with her head in her hands, crying out to God. Suddenly, Jesus appeared before her and sang her a love song:

> *When you are walking through the valley, I'll lead you.*
> *On the fatness of the land, I will feed you.*

After Jesus finished singing this song, He backed out through the same wall He

The Church Within the Church

had come in through, proving to Phyllis that He would never ever turn His back on her. That made such an impact on her life that she was never the same again. She knew from that day forward that there was nothing she could not get through and that the Lord would be right beside her at all times.

He was there with her in 2000, when her husband passed away. He was there with her in 2003, when she laid her mother to rest. He was there in 2013 when, in the course of three months, she lost a brother, a brother-in-law, and two sisters-in-law. And He kept her through it all.

It has been Jesus' everlasting love that has propelled Phyllis onward, to press toward the mark of the high calling in Christ Jesus. It is in Him that she lives and moves and has her being.

You may contact the author at:

Phyllis Harper Isenhart
1861 Pony Farm Road, Lot 4
Jacksonville, NC 28540
or
p.isenhart47@gmail.com

My father in 1956 talking with some of his parishioners at a church he pastored for about 15 years

Rock of Zion OFWB Church in Grantsboro, North Carolina, the church we attended when Dad was not preaching somewhere else

Other Books by Phyllis Harper Isenhart

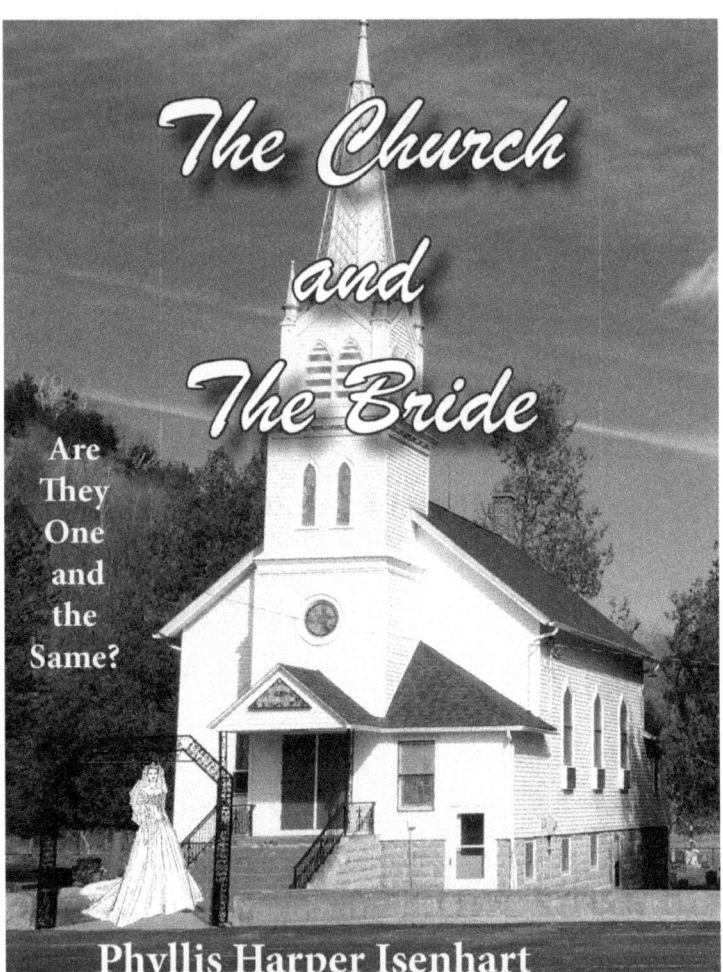

Where the River Flows

Phyllis Harper Isenhart

www.ingramcontent.com/pod-product-compliance
Lightning Source LLC
Chambersburg PA
CBHW032207040426
42449CB00005B/477